Bluewater Walkabout

Into the Caribbean

Tina Dreffin
Blue Publishing, Inc

DISCLAIMER

All the stories in this book are true, although some names and identifying details have been changed to protect the privacy of the people involved.

To all my readers...

Sorry about that last cliff-hanger in "Bluewater Walkabout: Into Africa". I'll buy you a Kalik beer when you reach the Bahamas to make up for it. I promise! Call me VHF #79.

May you find your big adventure on the high seas
and set that wild side of you free.

CONTENTS

Preface vii

1: Come Play With Me 1

2: Dog & Dolphin Wrestle 5

3: The Distracted Zen of Fishing 11

4: Shark Bait 15

5: Red Hot Invaders 19

6: Dancing With A Stingray 23

7: Sea Heart 27

8: Night Shock 31

9: The Diabless 35

10: Turtle Jump-Up 39

11: The San Blas Islands 43

12: Sunset Bliss 49

13: Become A Minimalist 53

About Tina Dreffin 57

PREFACE

The Dreffin Family

This book is a collection of short stories, penned during the years I cruised from the Bahamas to the Windward and Leeward Islands in the Caribbean with my husband and two sons.

Originally, these anecdotes were published in the Caribbean Compass Newspaper as articles and distributed in the Caribbean islands.

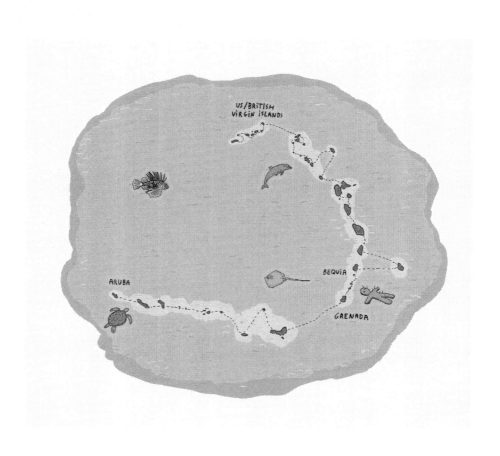

I
Come Play With Me

Nikki

We do not inherit the Earth from our ancestors, we borrow it from our children.

—Native American Proverb

We were anchored in Exuma, Bahamas, aboard *Scud*, our 45' steel monohull, in turquoise waters clear as air. Onboard were my husband, Peter, and our two young sons: Adam 9, and Warren, age 8.

The boys' merry prattle lent a cadence to which I listened with pleasure as they completed afternoon school lessons closely. They were happy to have finally reached the Bahamas after our eventful passage down the US East Coast and Gulfstream River.

In the cockpit, I breathed in the ocean breeze, scented with frangipani

1

and took in the stunning view of harbor waters against the backdrop of island cays. I was filled with languid melancholy.

Soon, though, I was brought out of my quiet reverie when an odd sound erupted against the boat, apparently coming from the bow.

Thump, thump.

Curious, I sauntered forward on deck with the boys in quick pursuit behind me. Together we peered over the side, but nothing seemed amiss. The eerie sound came again. This time we ran forward to peer over the bow....no, nothing, again.

"Mommy!" shouted Warren animatedly and then added, "Look!"

He pointed towards the waters where a slight ripple vibrated across the surface, then disappeared as fast as it had come.

"There!" screamed Adam. He stabbed his forefinger towards the depths of the sea, further down along the hull.

A dark shaped lingered in shadows and then raced underneath our twin hulls, silent as a torpedo, and just as fast.

We rushed astern. The boys chorused, "Daddy!"

Peter tossed aside his tools below-decks and ambled into the cockpit with his usual calm, confident repose. The boys were revving into overdrive: A blurry wave of arms and legs pin wheeled as they surged around the boat, following the dolphin.

Robin, our Belgium barge dog (widely known as a Schipperke), grew anxious from the tease of the mermaid in the waters below. The heightened cacophony of the boys' squeals together with the dog's hysteria was comical.

All at once, the dark shape shot out of the water, dove for the heavens, slid back down from the clouds, and somersaulted into a back flip, entering the waters at the exact spot it had exited.

A hushed silence fell over the boat.

"Mommy, it's a dolphin!" Warren squealed.

The dolphin streamlined back to the bow, and proceeded to rub her back along the anchor rode. She circled the boat, and returned to the bow to use the anchor road as a massage tool...over and over again. We stared wide-eyed, mouths ajar as we scurried across the decks, following her hypnotic sashaying around the boat.

Quickly, we grabbed our mask and fins to slither into the waters, careful not to alarm the dolphin. Before taking the plunge, Peter and I eyed the children: Big white saucers blinked back at us from behind masks like twin headlights. The hot summer breeze was heavy with their unspoken words of eager anticipation, nerves vibrating like drum skins. In the waters, Adam hung close to Peter's side and Warren was nearly upon my back.

We hung back out of respect for the wild mammal, giving her ample room. With waters clear as cellophane, details were sharp on her shiny skin: a slight scar ran across the dorsal fin and inconspicuous barnacle scrapes stretched along her snow-white underbelly.

We followed the dolphin's movements as she frolicked close-by, dipping and rising to the surface, never really going anywhere. She emitted a single-toned squeal to convey alarm to us – or possibly excitement. The click that projected from the melon on her forehead acted as a sonar beam, bouncing off *Scud's* hulls to guide her away. The beam enabled her to avoid collision with us and no doubt the dolphin herd when she swam fast, up to 25 mph. Typically, we saw dolphins as they traveled in small herds of 5-10, yet up to an immense school of 1,000 when we've crossed oceans.

In the shallow waters, the dolphin darted between us, stopping to pause two feet in front of the boys, barrel-rolling across the sandy bottom. If she swam too far into the glassy void, the boys back-peddled to the safety of Mom and Dad. Sensing a disappearing audience, the dolphin turned back to tease the boys out again.

For two hours the dolphin played cat and mouse and we grew weary. Her finale touched all our hearts though.

The dolphin swam up to the boys in shallow water. She was so close that Warren propelled himself out of the waters as if in sheer freight. The dolphin did likewise, breaking the surface like a rocket bent on speed alongside him, over half her body pointing to the heavens.

Warren and the dolphin met in mid-air amidst a face-off of sheer joy. In the late afternoon light, the dolphin's glistening form towered over Warren's tiny frame.

Over the next few days, the dolphin returned to our boat for her daily massage on the anchor rode. We never did figure out where she came from, or why she seemed so tame. We named her Nikki, for the little nick in her back, possibly from a close encounter with an angry shark.

We have long considered the presence of dolphins that cruised alongside our bows as a good omen and a promise of fair weather. Many classical writers have described how dolphins were once harnessed to chariots to help maidens in distress.

We considered Nikki our lucky talisman, a gift to continue our wandering cruise down the island chain of the Caribbean, forever ready for our next big adventure. No one back home would believe it. At least this time, we had the photo to prove it!

2
DOG & DOLPHIN WRESTLE

Nikki and Bella

We have more to learn from animals, than animals from us.
—Anthony D Williams

I awakened with a start. A familiar sound echoed through the twin hulls of our catamaran, dubbed *Freebird*, a 42' Grainger. Clambering out of the berth, I dashed up a set of stairs and tumbled into the cockpit, landing in a messy heap. I pulled myself up to see my husband, Peter, bending in half, nearby. He stood on the sugar-scoop end of the port hull, peering into turquoise waters clear as gin. We were anchored in the pristine waters of Exuma, Bahamas – the preferred waters for bottlenose dolphins.

"Is it her?" I shouted.

"Yes! And two more!" Peter said.

"Let's go then! Our buddy is back!"

I donned mask and snorkel, grabbed my underwater video camera, and dove into Elizabeth Harbor. As soon as I broke surface waters, three fins sped towards me. My heart thudded into my ears.

If I didn't know better, I could easily become bait since the fins closely resembled the most feared predator of the sea – the shark. But in actuality, I knew my friends had come to play with Bella, our little black Schipperke dog. I was the resident cheerleader. The promised show was about to start.

SPLASH!

Bella launched off the back of our catamaran and landed in a belly flop right behind me. Underwater, her short legs churned waters like a paddlewheel. She sprinted ahead of me and met the dolphins head on. In a dramatic display of roiling waves, the dolphins and dog collided. Squeaks and barks resounded across still waters.

I languished, simply treading water while taking in the scene. The dolphins were here to be entertained by us and we were eager to show them a good time.

Bella was overcome with excitement. She galloped towards the biggest dolphin, keeping a sharp lookout for the shape beneath the water. The dolphins swam in circles around her. Bella chased after them, yelping with glee.

I knew I had to keep Bella close to the boat; otherwise, she'd have me trailing her for miles. My dog was bent on chasing those dolphins, taking me to China – if I let her. She was actually afraid of the the dolphin. She'd be gifted many chances to ride on their backs, but always refused it out of respect…or confusion…or terror. Nikki often posed still, inches in front of Bella and yet, the dog never boarded her back.

"Bella, come!" I shouted. At my beckon, Bella turned and swam back towards me. So did the dolphin. When Bella reached me by the boat, the dolphin finned beneath Bella and stopped short a mere foot from her belly. Underwater, it looked as if the dolphin was standing on her tail in three feet of shallow water.

When the great beast performed a 360-degree spin on her tail and came toward me, my heart raced wildly. I dove down to meet her and stopped on the seafloor to wait. I wanted the beautiful beast to take the initiative, giving her loads of space. After all, it was a wild mammal, one to be respected and revered.

The dolphin slowly approached at face level. Her liquid blue eyes bored into my soul on the approach. When she halted directly in front of my face only inches away, it appeared as if we were having a virtual conversation with our minds. Her eyes seemed to be saying: "Hello. Thanks for playing with me."

I reached out to touch her —an irresistible urge. She was so close that her snout alone filled the frame of my wind-angled viewfinder.

By then, Bella was upon us, and the dolphin finned away to wreak havoc with the dog. The beast circled Bella three times, dolphin-tail dragging sideways across surface waters, just inches from Bella's snout.

Suddenly, the dolphin darted down three-feet into the shallow waters, plucked a blade of turtle grass from the seafloor, surfaced, and tossed it at Bella. The blade landed on Bella's snout and fell into the waters where it floated, and then started to slowly sink. The dolphin finned after the blade, grabbing it in her snout, and swam over to Bella where she tossed it at Bella again.

The dog went berserk. Bella barked and stroked fiercely, trying to catch the shiny fin that always remained just out of reach.

Suddenly the cat and mouse game ended and the dolphin sped to the bottom, performing a 360-degree flip. I knew what was coming when I saw her powerful tail jet her forward toward the surface.

With one last powerful stroke of her tail, she soared up, up, and up. Shooting to the surface, she bolted out of the water like a rocket, and executed a dizzying somersault over the black canine. When she landed, the end of her tail flicked, sending a wet whack right across Bella's snout.

Bella's eyes went wide with fury. Tiny black feet churned waters ever harder to catch the beast that plagued her.

This time when the dolphin darted back down again to the bottom to repeat the act, she blasted out of the sea on the opposite side of Bella, somersaulted over her, and went down again.

Three times the magnificent beast somersaulted over Bella. Poor Bella changed directions to meet her every time, only to be tricked when the dolphin sneaked up from behind her to execute jumps. I couldn't stop laughing. Dog and dolphin were wrestling at play.

Underwater, I heard other dolphins whistle, their calls long and melodious. Nikki replied with rapid burst pulse calls.

In time, I saw them coming. They rejoined their comrade and finned nearby, scouting scallops across the sandy bottom. Soon, shifting sands swirled around their snouts like tiny clouds as they drilled into tiny holes for crustaceans.

After another long period of dog and dolphin wrestle, I saw that my trusty dog was dangerously becoming overwhelmed. She couldn't control her appetite of engaging with the dolphins. No wonder too, they were quite a tease, this group.

Bella's signs of exhaustion were panting, frothing at the mouth, and violent shaking. When I held her in my arms, her heart raced wildly. It was time to end this game of cat and mouse. There's always another day.

I felt blessed to be invited to play with these magical creatures in the wild. Peter refuses to step into a zoo. Seeing gorgeous animals in captivity sends him into a fury. No wonder.

But times are changing for the better. Scientists are recommending that dolphins are so intelligent they should be given the same status as humans. Experts say it is now time for dolphins to be treated as 'non-human persons' after research showed their brains to have many features associated with high intelligence. They claim it is cruel to keep such intelligent animals in amusement parks.

Lori Marino, a zoologist at Emory University in Atlanta, studied MRI scans to map the brains of dolphins. Her studies revealed that many dolphin brains are larger than our own. The cerebral cortex and the neocortex of bottlenose dolphins were so large that "the anatomical ratios that assess cognitive capacity place it second only to the human brain".

When we swim with the dolphins, I identified three main types of sounds: echolocation clicks, burst pulse calls and whistles.

Echolocation clicks are used to sense their environment. These I hear when Nikki approaches our boat. She uses burst pulse calls for social communication when in an aggressive situation, like a warning shot for danger to her group. But the most call I hear is the whistle.

Whistles are much like our own and are used for social communication when in friendly interactions. Each dolphin has their own signature whistle, which is like saying their own name. Whistles are used when dolphins become separated and are trying to reunite with particular individuals.

I recognized Nikki's signature whistle immediately after hearing it over the years since we've know her. Her calls are a short buzzing sound followed by a high whistle and then a rapid buzz, much like a bumble bee following a hummingbird. Shirr. Zip, zip. Bella can hear the calls below-decks, but I can only hear them when in the water.

This family of dolphins has resided in these waters of Exuma for thirty years or more. Since we reared our sons here, they have known these dolphins since as young boys.

Ever since that first day of dolphin play years ago, Nikki has been regular a visitor around our boat. She seems to locate us whenever we change anchorages. We often encounter her en route during our regular morning swim too.

Now, when Nikki fins by to romp with our little black dog, she often brings her baby to show off. We dubbed the baby dolphin, Heloise. The beau – daddy of Heloise – rarely approaches. So being more standoffish, we never got around to naming him. It's best that way. I prefer him to be the protector of the group.

Aboard *Freebird*, I have a beach décor sign that reads:
ADVICE FROM A DOLPHIN
Have a playful spirit. Be curious. Find someone you click with. Sound out new ideas. Glide through the day with ease. Find your life's porpoise. Jump for joy!

I read it every day, forever appreciative that I live aboard a boat with my honey and regularly swim with dolphins in turquoise waters clear as mountain air.

We've been bluewater cruising for thirty-five years now. Each year is better than the last, thanks to the dolphins. They still come – up to five now.

3
THE DISTRACTED ZEN OF FISHING

Adam & Warren with a Mahi-Mahi

Parents don't take pictures of their kids playing video games.
They take them when fishing.

—Tina Dreffin

We were on passage from St. Martin to St. Lucia aboard *Scud*, our St. Francis 44' catamaran. We hadn't snagged a fish after an entire morning of waiting, waiting, waiting. Beans and rice are the norm of our diet, being largely vegetarian, but enough Mexican and green stuff - we wanted fresh catch-of-the-day.

"Why haven't we caught one yet?" I asked Adam, our handsome 15-yr old son, official angler expert. In addition to his brother, Warren (age 14), both were reared on boats in the Caribbean. They are well-know for their hand-crafted lures, constructed from pink and yellow plastic bags, foraged from island markets.

"I'll check the lures, in case we snagged seaweed," Adam said rather inattentively. Odd, since normally, he's intensely focused on the status of his rig—the set and proper boat speed to land a fish.

"Sweet!" Warren exclaimed animatedly as he appeared in the open doorway of our cockpit.

Turning forward, I followed their gazes—my eyes danced with merriment. *Scud* was overtaking a big charter cat where a Sheila artfully posed on the stern, donned in an itsy-bitsy-teeny-weeny, neon-pink bikini, and combing her blond hair. Long tendrils streamed behind her in the stiff breeze as the cat gently lurched forward in the light chop. Wild Leopard trumpeted in large golden letters across her quarters.

Peter, a stealthy tactician, tightened his grip on the helm to out-ma-neuver and overtake her. Sheets were tweaked as his eyes twinkled with the thrill of the chase.

"She's definitely a TEN!" The guys chorused together.

The cat or the Pink Bikini? I wondered.

Warren launched onto the other sugar-scoop to join Adam as *Scud* charged Wild Leopard, a formidable prey. We'd stolen their wind! There would be hell to pay for outwitting the king of the seas.

Once coming abreast of the cat, the boys languished astern. Sun glistened off their toned bodies, earned from years of challenging water-sports. The boys posed for Pink Bikini, angling this way. Ah, the antics of the young. I made sure Peter focused on the helm and not the stunning Sheila flashing our way.

Soon, we left the charter cat in our wake, floundering in dead air. We plunged forward, *Scud* like the steeple-chaser she was. Scenic coves fringed in palms, silhouetted against towering verdant pitons, drifted by.

"Hey guys," I said merrily, "you know—dinner. A fish? Did you do the chat?"

Their High School courses had included the philosophical hunting precepts acquired from Buddhism and the North American Indians. They taught one to cultivate compassion for all animals, to ask for your gift from Mother Nature, and then apologize to the kill when acquired, thanking it for coming.

So we gave it a go: Gazing up into the azure blue sky and cobalt-blue sea, pushing forward loving intent, asking for a fish to feed our family.

After our little chat with the Universe, we forgot about it and Pink Bikini. Very soon, though, the clothespin alarm went flinging across the cockpit, smacking Adam in the face. The line raced into the depths of the sea with an energy all its own.

We promised to follow the universal laws of protecting the oceans: save our trash until landfall, catch only legal-sized fish. We whispered how we loved the waters—the dour smiling groupers, the playful dolphins that darted across our bows. We promised to steadfastly protect the oceans, standing tall to defend it. Last, we sent appreciation for the fish we hoped to land, and especially for the opportunity of being here, in this moment, sailing in paradise.

"We got a fish!" Adam yelled.

Much shouting, pulling, yanking, and rushing about ensued in landing the fish. Once aboard, its size was impressive. With a blessing this size, it was meant to be shared.

I spoke gently to the magnificent mahi-mahi, thanking it for coming. "Be still, sweet one. You are splendid in your colors. Don't suffer," I cooed. Suddenly, it went quiet and its life gently receded.

Adam proudly held up our prize on the stern as I shot the photo. In the viewfinder, I noticed *Wild Leopard* sneaking up close behind. She'd gained the advantage when we'd slowed to land the fish. As they passed, Adam held aloft his prize to the onlookers onboard the charter cat. They exploded in applause as Pink Bikini waved earnestly. Adam's grin split his face in two.

"When we reach port guys," I said, "we'll invite them to join us." Two beauties at the table are far better than one.

4
SHARK BAIT

Nurse Sharks

Fear is only temporary. Regret lasts forever.

—Tina Dreffin

I wouldn't go in there, if I were you," warned the dock-master. We were at the Virgin Islands marina gas dock.

Peter and I were poised to tie up our dinghy, needing gas for our jerry cans. Donned in wetsuits, we planned to free-dive for conch on the outer reef.

Before clambering out of the dinghy, I stared down with interest at the nine nurse sharks resting in the shallows below. They weren't really going anywhere. Just hanging out.

"What are they waiting for?" I asked a friendly West Indian who was standing beside me.

"De' food mon, when the divers come in to clean de' fish. They go bananas!" he added.

Jerry cans can wait. This could be fun, I thought. After grabbing a mask and snorkel, I slipped a GoPro into my suit and slid into waters as clear as gin, throwing caution to the wind.

"Stay close," I told Peter. He rolled his eyes at me, used to my crazy ways.

In eight feet of water, I gazed down in amazement as eight brown nurse sharks fingered the sand with large pectoral fins as if they were 'walking' along the ocean floor. Swimming in close to a particularly comatose seven-footer, its head turned to eye me warily. I eased into reverse gear, giving it more respect – and more space.

Nice puppy, I cooed.

Taking refuge in the shadow of the drifting dinghy, I allowed the current to take me over two other nurse sharks. They were busy feeding on small marine invertebrates: crabs, sea urchins or snails hidden in the sand. Fortunately for me, human flesh is not included in their diet – a small comfort to stupid American tourists, like moi.

Out of my peripheral vision, I caught a juvenile male torpedoing my way, much closer to the surface than the others. Alarmed, I sped over to the dinghy that had drifted away. The curious shark was close behind. Once I grasped the dinghy handle, I gave a fierce kick, and launched myself onto the wet floor.

"Having fun dear?" Peter said, a wide grin spreading across his face. I love it when he teased me.

"Not to worry," I replied coolly with more confidence than I felt.

Nurse sharks – often known as sand tigers – are sluggish in daylight hours, becoming more active at night when they congregate in larger numbers to feed. They won't attack unless provoked but they can be dangerous. Nurse sharks have been recorded as having attacked only 23 people during the last four centuries. Out of 42 different species of sharks, they come 8th in line of attacks worldwide, behind the hammerhead (31), bull shark (69), tiger shark (104), and great white (311). Who's counting when it's me in the water?

But I know the nurse shark knows that I'm there. Acute eyesight enabled a shark to locate me at night in murky waters. It can sniff me out one-quarter mile away with powerful sensors – I was a few feet at the moment. Sharks are sensitive to movement and can detect weak electrical charges through pores in their skin, enabling them to hunt buried prey at night.

No more nighttime skinny-dipping for me, even if it is beside the boat during a full moon, calypso music across still waters, coconut palms swaying ...

I have compassion for all sharks. Snorkeling in their habitat has brought me great pleasure though not all would agree. Ill-informed fishermen kill sharks intentionally, believing their catch is lessened. Thousands die in fishing nets each year. Humans hunt sharks for sport, food (shark-fin soup is prized in Southeast Asia) and medicine. Shark liver oil is supplemented for vitamin A, the cartilage extracted for cancer cures, skins tanned for shoes, handbags, and belts. Little regard is given for the health of shark populations. According to NOAA Fisheries, over 100 million sharks are killed each year needlessly. I'll continue to enjoy the healthy shark populations in the Caribbean, jumping in from time-to-time to get up close and personal.

5
RED HOT INVADERS

Look, But Don't Touch the Invasive Lionfish

Only those who will risk going too far can possibly find out how far one can go.

—*T. S. Eliot*

It was my turn. Peter, my husband, was snorkeling below our dinghy. I like to go in last, just so he can tell me if Jaws is lurking about. Once given the 'thumbs up', I plunged in and saw below me fuchsia-tipped sea anemone wriggling in crystalline, turquoise-blue waters, and a dwarf sea horse shimmying along the skinny branches of a purple gorgonian that undulated in the current.

I began to relax. It had been a fast and furious 10-day passage from

Florida to the Virgin Islands. We had sailed together onboard *Scud*, our St. Francis 44' catamaran.

Suddenly, I was snapped out of my musings when Peter's eyes went wide inside the frame of his face mask. With his forefinger, he gesticulated at a gargantuan coral-head, twenty-feet below us on the sea floor, and then motioned for me to free-dive down. I was taken aback, but then, upon further reflection, he was the one clutching the spear for Jaws. For you know who, just in case...

Feeling apprehensive, I peered around me and then down into the busy reef for possible signs of trouble. A foolishly smiling parrot fish grazed on elkhorn coral and a large turtle darted by in alarm, its flippers fueling fast, obviously upset with our intrusion. My hackles rose, but I still couldn't find what gave rise to Peter's concern. All appeared happy and content inside the Caribbean Explorer Channel to me. Yet something was there ... Snorkeling in the Virgins is always an adventure, and today looked to be unlike any other.

"There!" he mumbled into his snorkel, words coming out garbled, like his mouth was loaded with web marbles. Tiny bubbles whirled from his mouthpiece. I finned down for a closer look, bypassing a myriad of tropical fish that resembled sparkling jewels in the brilliant sunlight. In a dark void beneath the colossal coral head, I peered to see not one, but two of the most voracious predators of the sea, the *pterois volitans* — fearless red lion fish. Like lightening, I swirled backwards, whirling into a reverse turbo-charged spin.

Geez! I gulped, heart pounding in years. These guys definitely required respect.

Lionfish are stunning to watch, but don't touch. "You'll want to die," whispered my Caribbean friend Diane, over a lunch of conch burgers at the Red Hot Mamma afterwards. Surely she was kidding, I thought. Then, with bulging yes, she leaned in towards me, and described how she had been stung while shelling off a remote sandbar. Bent double in pain, she chewed on wood as her sister poured hot water over her foot, the recommended treatment for drawing out poison.

"I found a magnificent shell though!" she beamed at me. That's the spirit of the islands here.

It's not only humans who regard the formidable lionfish warily. Armed with eighteen billowy fins, lionfish paralyze their prey with venomous spines, then suck them down in one violent gulp — fins, scales, and all.

With an alien face, the lionfish resembles my grandmother's hatpin cushion, shredded by a rogue Rottweiler. Slight comfort to know they don't eat humans. No one has perished from lionfish stings, either.

Where did they come from? Lionfish are native to warm Indo-Pacific waters. It's believed they were accidentally swept into the Atlantic thirteen years ago from aquariums when Hurricane Andrew ravaged Florida. Others are intentionally related by well-meaning private aquarium owners after "Finding Nemo" hit the box office. Few are aware of the negative impact that an invasive species can cause on native fish like lobster, group, and snapper.

Lionfish are rapidly expanding into the Caribbean at an alarming pace. Governments are very worried. Possessed of a voracious appetite, a single lionfish can devour up to twenty juvenile fish in a half hour. On one experimental reef, juveniles were reduced by 80 percent in five weeks. Often, these are native fish species critical to tourism and fishing industries.

Lionfish also display an impressive reproductive rate. An adult female can release a pair of egg sacs five times each month, laying as many as 30,000 eggs several times, year-round. Veteran dive operators have warned that it could be the worst ecological disaster the world has ever experienced. One expert compared the lionfish to a "plague of locusts".

As a result, may recreational divers are removing lionfish from the reef. Like, "kill them on sight?" I asked Diane. She happens to be a naturalist, working to protect her island's natural marine resources.

"You have to kill them! Grouper are only now beginning to recover from the over-fishing of the 1970s and '80s," she insisted. I gulped. I'm a real chicken when it comes to squaring off with a lion.

"People eat venomous fish in Southeast Asia. Maybe it takes good?" I questioned Diane, hoping she'd let me off the hook of scoring a lionfish.

"Skinning a pin cushion would be fun to see," Diane laughed with a glint in her eye.

Today, I'm off to hunt the fearsome predator of the deep, clad in full wetsuit, hood, and gloves. I'm hesitant. I follow the Buddhist practice of abstaining from harmful acts against nature. So, upon reflection, I think I'll just snap a photo. Maybe the lionfish will establish harmony with the reef, and become a creature to be respected, instead of feared and destroyed.

This may already be happening. The stomachs of several groupers have been found containing remnants of lionfish, establishing hope that "native grouper species are beginning to prey on red lionfish with some regularity", as reported by Simon Fraser, University's Tropical Marine Lab, recently.

6
DANCING WITH A STINGRAY

Dancing Stingrays

The ocean stirs the heart, inspires the imagination, and brings eternal joy to the soul.

—*Robert Wyland*

The curvy beach on Anguilla seemed like the perfect spot for a luxurious saltwater bath. An islander stood at one end doing something unusual with large shells. So I sauntered towards the opposite end for my bath.

My attempt at calling in the rain with a jig on deck failed, so with shampoo and liquid Quell in hand, I took the plunge.

A myriad of fuzzy colors enveloped my vision underwater. I let myself go for a long period, relaxing in turquoise-blue waters, clear as mountain air.

Getting on with the business at hand, I finned into the shallows, and standing with legs splayed wide for balance against the slight surf, proceeded to shampoo my hair. Feeling 'in the groove', I twisted mid-length strands into an impressive lather, shaping them into tall spikes, and gnarly dreadlocks while barreling out "zippa-de-do-dah..."

"Mind your feet, lady!" shouted the islander behind me on the beach.

How had I drifted down towards him so fast?

Shoving aside a bubbly spike of bangs, I squinted with one open eye to see him yanking out a fleshy snail from a queen conch. A gaggle of lobster-red tourists, were clustered around behind him.

I became alarmed when a stifled cry came from one of the women. Suddenly, I felt something soft and slimy glide between my legs. Clawing at the soap in the other eye, I got the shock of my life when I peered down to see a large grey shape undulate between my feet.

A giant stingray!

What the heck?

The surprise caused me to lose my balance. I tumbled backwards onto a pile of holed conch shells, litter from the conch man. Ouch. With legs flailing, I tried to disentangle myself, keeping a sharp lookout for the stingray.

Hungry, the stingray cruised the beach for leftover conch bits as I gazed in wonder. Satiated, but wanting more, the stingray torpedoed into a rhumb-line for the conch pile behind me.

"Watch out!" Conchman shouted.

I quickly gathered my wits and tried to stand, but my bikini bottom had snagged on the conch shells. Extricating my suit would've taken only a second, but seconds I didn't have.

"Catch!" Conchman shouted again. He launched himself into an Olympian roll of the shoulder, pitching conch entrails at me. Gooey guts flew through the air, misty slime spinning off like raindrops. I caught the wet mass, not sure of what to do next.

"Feed it to him," he shouted.

SAY WHAT?

Clutching the guts by the foot, I shoved them underwater at the eager stingray. It slithered slowly towards me, then stopped at my entangled legs to feed on my proffered entrée-of-the-day. As entrails were vacuumed from a ventral mouth, the head bobbed up and down, and swirling sands billowed out from beneath giant wing-like pectoral fins.

Then something weird happened – the ray partially slithered onto my lap, looking for more.

What do I do? Newspaper headlines blasted in my numb brain of: "Yachtswoman Dies in Shallows from Sea Creature" or "Sea Monster Electrocutes Woman".

"Don't move! Mind the tail!" shouted Conchman. He tossed me more entrails. "Hold it under the snout!"

The red tourists, oohed and aahhed, snapping digital photos in rapid succession.

Ever so slowly I placed my open palm beneath the head of the ray, offering it as a token for my life. "Nice kitty. Please go home to mommy," I cooed in pleading tones. My Buddhist nature screamed trouble: I don't believe in harassing or taming sea life. This is nuts!

The ray nuzzled my palm, caressing my fingers with soft, velvety lips – like those of a sweet-natured mare. A pleasant tingling sensation rose, rushing up my forearm. I simply smiled. After poking around for more, the ray swirled around to retreat, whipping a bulbous tail across my trembling feet. I froze, not wanting to startle it with any sudden movement.

This is NOT recommended behavior. Petting or feeding rays encourages human approach The long, whip-like tail of a stingray can inflict severe wounds – stingrays are, in fact, the most common cause of severe fish stings. The barbed spines at the base of the tail contain poisonous glands, utilized as a defense mechanism against predators.

In addition, stingrays are fascinating creatures. Aboard *Scud*, my husband, Peter, and I see them often. In quiet anchorages, we hear them as they catapult from water into mid-air, landing with a thunderous clap. We dash on deck to watch the show, feeling euphoric with their repeated performance.

When snorkeling, we see them feeding on mollusks and crustaceans in shallows: We know they are near when broken conch shell shards litter the ocean floor or when a cloud of whirling sands emerges before us, making navigation difficult. We give them a wide berth, not wanting to disturb them, then turn to admire their fluttering ballet as they glide through still waters.

Swimming alongside a pair of leopard rays is a mystical experience.

Once, as a young girl while snorkeling with my Dad, I was astonished to gaze below me and discover a multitude of eyes blinking back at me from the ocean floor: a school of rays at rest, blanketed in sand for protection against predators.

Next time I decide to wallow in shallows with soapy spikes, I'll don a face mask to maintain a sharp look-out for lovely sea creatures of the deep – just in case adventure comes drifting my way when I least expect it.

7
SEA HEART

Sea Beans from Around the World

I am a drifter and as lonely as that can be, it is also remarkably freeing.

—David Levithan

My friend raced down the beach in Orient Bay of St. Martin like a mare with her tangled blond mane streaming behind her. Taken aback, I charged after her, considering my new cruising buddy to be in dire need of help. Had she been stung by a bee? Seen a child sink beneath the waves, caught in tidal current?

We were discussing the merits of extended cruising while our husbands traded outboard engine life-saving techniques at a street side café nearby. Suddenly, Debbie launched into overdrive, nose to the sands.

After a distance, Debbie halted in her tracks, bent forward into a stunning yoga pose and retrieved a faultless sea heart from the high water tide mark. Arms stretched to the blue heavens with fingertips wriggling, she shouted, "Thank-you!"

Her exclamation resounded into the bar and cafes, street shops, and homes alongside the road. Curious bystanders stopped to view the commotion.

A sea heart! My heart soared – good fortune strikes the lucky person who finds one so near to St. Valentines Day.

Sea hearts are an augury of better things to come and for safe passages – the perfect gift for a lady of the sea. Debbie happened to be cruising the Caribbean for the first time on *Island Fever*, a Lagoon 42'.

It is said that a sea heart gave Columbus the inspiration to sail west from Europe in search of new sea-routes to Asia. When embarking upon long ocean voyages, the sea hearts were worn by his crew as amulets and called favas de Colum or Columbus beans. Sailors believed they would be protected from evil spirits and illness if they wore the heart. The bean can survive long perilous journeys across oceans for years.

Sea hearts are more widely known as sea beans or drift seeds. Coconuts and tropical almonds are larger examples of drift seeds. The smaller sea hearts originate as seeds inside large pods of a wild tropical vine, like those found in the Amazon River Basin and other verdant rain forests around the world. Clusters of blossoms dangle from upper rainforest canopies where they are easily accessed by night-flying bats. The bats sip the sweet nectar, transferring the pollen to other plants.

Once pollination occurs, the ovary of each flower develops into a legume pod containing several larges seeds. Some resemble hearts, others miniature hamburgers because of the attachment scar from the vine. The tropical vines twine through the forest canopy like botanical boa constrictors, creating monkey ladders – arboreal thoroughfares for forest animals. Because of the intense competition between plants for space and light, the monkey ladder can quickly climb to heights of 100' or more in just 18 months. Monkeys, sloths, lizards, and snakes become adept trapeze artists of the forest by using it.

Once the giant velvety legume pods produce the large, heart-shaped seeds, hurricane force winds force them out of the pod and onto the forest floor, where gullies and creeks collect them at the high water mark and carry them out to sea. Because of their hard, thick, woody seed coat, the seeds are impervious to water, and internal air cavities makes them buoyant, allowing them to ride ocean currents for years to any distant port. Due to strong Caribbean ocean currents, thousands of drift seeds are found each year on beaches in Florida, the UK, and Europe.

Not only are sea-beans symbols of good luck, they have a multitude of medicinal purposes. The bean pods contain the brain neurotransmitter dopamine, which is given to patients suffering from Parkinson's' Disease. Male and female seeds from one particular rain forest liana are believed to prevent hemorrhoids, carried by natives in the Amazon River Basin between villages. They have been ground into a poultice to relieve painful inflammations and taken internally for contraception, constipation, snake bits, or as an aphrodisiac. Village women use it as a shampoo or laundry soap.

Few Caribbean ports are without these lovely sea-beans: in Belize they are called *ojo de buey* (eye of the bull) by local residents. West Indian policemen once used them as billy-clubs. In the Andes, enchanting rhythms waft across night breezes from musical sea-bean shakers. In Dominica, the giant drift seeds are used as an ornamental shaker gourd. I've seen them used as rosaries at Catholic mass and sold as stunning necklaces and bracelets in Jamaica, as well as throughout the Caribbean.

A week later, I caught up with Debbie at the local farmers' market. From her neck dangled a lacquered sea-heart that glistened brightly in the morning sunlight. Little did I know that good fortune awaited me as I later strolled down the beach, nose to the sands. My prize: A St. Mary's sea-bean, considered rare amongst beach combers as only one in 1,000 is ever found. On the face rests a perfectly formed crucifix, a symbol for faith, hope, and love for the New Year.

8
NIGHT SHOCK

Morning Entree': Frittata with Flying Fish

Let your hook be always cast. In the pool where you least expect it, will be fish.

—Ovid

When on passage, shocking events always seem to occur in the blackness of night. I never know when or if they are coming. I can't look out for them.

Whenever off-watch, white saucer-eyes bulge from my face when I imagine all the bizarre happenings that are possible. I stare up at the cabin overhead, unable to slam shut my eyelids. My imagination goes beyond out-of-control. Relax. Nothing will happen. Go to sleep.

But then—something always does happen.

After sailing 100,000 nautical miles, I don't believe won't happen. Today, I believe in truth. It has definitely set me free.

My first incident with night shock came on a moonless night when heavy cloud cover obliterated the stars, creating a black void of sea and sky. Peter and I were sailing south from the big island of Dominica to St Lucia onboard *Antilles*, a 46' Sparkman and Stevens wooden ketch that we owned many years ago.

While sailing in the wind shadow of Dominica, my night watch was magical. Lights winked at me from the coastline and the rich aroma of wood smoke rode the sea breeze.

When Peter assumed the helm for his watch, the gave me a passing kiss. We always embrace…just in case it's our last chance. Living aboard a boat for 20 years inspires it—appreciate every day as if it's your last.

Peter's watch would grow more remarkable in the Dominican Channel where unbridled seas rolled in from western Africa, currents whirled, and breezes grew blustery. I was happy to hand the wheel over, eagerly awaiting the comfort of my Concordia berth in the main salon.

Clambering into my sea berth, it grew hot and sticky, making it difficult to sleep. On this sultry night, I cranked open my porthole— against Peter's dire warnings. The sea breeze felt refreshing on my face. We were on a port tack, so I considered the window to be high enough that no spray would enter. How very wrong I was.

It came in the middle of my dreams, just at the good part when a calypso beat resounded against the backdrop of a full moon with my love in my arms…

Bam!

Something heavy smacked into my chest, taking my breath away and drawing me full awake. Confused, I thrust out my arms to shield against unseen blows. The blows came in repetitive rhythm. To block them, I thrust my forearms up and got it full in the face. What the …!

A foul odor replaced the sweet sea breeze. The monster on my chest flopped, writhed, and wriggled up and down my torso in a frenetic dance for its life. I shrieked a howl of terror and jumped out of the berth.

Hearing my screams, Peter engaged the wind vane and charged down the companionway, taking several stairs at a time and missing most. Clawing at the light, he feared the worst, but when it cast a beam on me, he let out a raucous laugh.

When I gazed down, I was shocked to see great silvery scales the size of nickels clinging to my skin. Atop my tummy somersaulted a colossal flying fish, fighting for its life. Peter engulfed the magnificent sea creature into his arms, and shoved the foot-long writhing mass back into the sea through the wide-open port-hole, securing it shut.

"Dancing with fate a little too close, my dear?" he chuckled with a twinkle in his eye. That's what I love about my Peter—he never loses his cool.

Years later, we were passage-making from Grenada to Puerto Rico aboard *Scud*. I was enjoying my dogwatch when a litany of expletives exploded into the night. Suddenly our son, Adam, bounded into the cockpit, howling with despair.

"I've been attacked... by a fish! AARGGH!" he wailed.

Recognizing the agony of night shock, I released a litany of uncontrolled guffaws, recalling my first time.

"It came at me through the hatch!" he hollered.

Clasping the monster by its tail, he gave a roll of the shoulder to pitch it into the sea, but I quickly grabbed it away from him.

"It's mine!" I implored. I'd made peace with the flying fish. It was my favorite morning entree' now—a real sailor's delicacy.

At daybreak, I took my flying fish into the galley. Over a breakfast of scrambled eggs and catch-of-the-day, family conversation was lively.

According to my Field Guides, the *Exocoetus volitans* was the most common species of flying fish. Pursued by hungry predators—like the bluefish or albacore—flying fish can swim rapidly and hang close to the surface, launching themselves into the air with a fierce whip of the tail to glide. With streamlined, elongated pectoral fins—appearing like wings—they are able to achieve the lift they needed to soar, gliding as far as 200 yards and lifting above the surface to a maximum of 36 feet. Flying fish in California have been measured as long as an impressive eighteen inches.

The fish is considered a coveted delicacy in Caribbean waters. Barbados was historically nicknamed land of the flying fish when flying fish were abundant around the island. They fed on the plankton-rich waters that swept up from the Orinoco River in Venezuela. Today, the flying fish regularly migrate to Tobago, becoming a culinary favorite, as well. In Barbados, the national dish is known as cou-cou.

The term *Exocoetidae* comes from the Greek, meaning sleeping under the stars and refers to the flying fish being stranded on boats.

Now when I hit the pillow off-watch at night, I'm donned in full battle gear of ball-cap, cookie sheet on my belly, and the most critical piece of all—a net.

9
THE DIABLESS

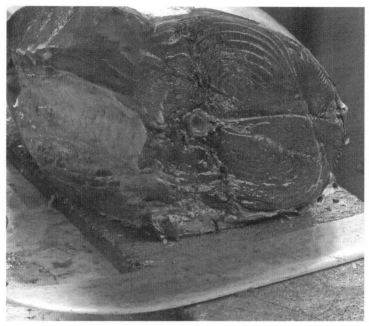

Tuna Vendors Are Full of Surprises

We travel not to escape life, but for life not to escape us.
—Anonymous

Yesterday I shopped at the farmers' and fish markets in St Georges, Grenada, while the boys completed their schoolwork. A patchwork of fruits and vegetables greeted me, many looking otherworldly—like the achiote from South America.

The seeds of achiote are ground and made into a red dye, formerly used by the Tainos Indians. Nicknamed *bija*, it delineated male virility and repelled mosquitoes. Culinary chefs used the achiote paste to flavor cuisines. I vowed to use it in my next curry.

An island woman towered over a mountain of vegetables and

beckoned me over. Biceps pushed at the sleeves of her floral blouse as hands the size of hams handled delicate tomatoes. A fedora shaded her face.

"Fresh tuna for you today?" the Grenadian woman asked as she whirled a machete in the air. Beside her lay a tuna, its tail drooping over the plank's edge. Vibrant eyes announced a recent kill. The price was shockingly low, so I grabbed two kilos.

I asked about the farming practices that Peter and I studied in the Grand Etang Rain Forest recently. The fish vendor shed light on the island's agricultural practices, handed down through generations.

"Foresters plant banana and plantain groves near cocoa trees to shelter the delicate plants from high winds and sun," the Tuna Lady said. "My husband, he does that too, in 'de back yard.'"

I showed Tuna Lady my treasure. "Ah, you found the red gold of Grenada," she hissed excitedly, sucking breath through brown teeth. "Wars have been fought over that treasure. It is the nutmeg. Before it came to dis island, de East India Spice Company kept it all to 'demselves and hid it in the Bantu Islands of Indonesia." She spat on the ground, revealing her disgust of the trickery.

She peeled off the encasing of the brown nut. "This red part here be the mace blade. Let it dry til it's yellow-orange in color and then use it like a bay leaf in de cooking. Take it out of de dish before you feed your mon. Grate the nut when it is dry. Follow dis' and your mon will follow you to de ends of de earth, girl!" She cackled, gold tooth flashing like beams of a Chevy.

"You have problem with your mon?" she asked, staring at me intently.

"Ah, no, not really. Well, he's distracted sometimes," I said.

"Oh then. You must see my sista'. She can make the diabless go away."

"The diabless?"

"Girl, don't you know? The diabless ..."

She leaned into me, garlic breath wafting, glancing around to ensure secrecy. "The diablesses are demonic women that come out to seduce your mon! Ah, yes, you must call on my sista'. She has special powers to help you."

"Ah, yeah, well..." I grabbed my parcel to sneak out. "Thanks anyway. Bye, now." My scalp tingled as I tossed coins on the table for my purchases and hurried off—imagining voodoo characters gathering to swoop down on me.

Tuna Lady's raucous guffaws echoed as tentacles of laughter clawed air and gave chase. I dashed awkwardly through the crowded market, ricocheting off natives, dropping half of my purchases. I watched disheartened as tomatoes and onions rolled down the hill, tumbling into gutter. I ran and ran, all the way until I waved down a jitney. I clambered aboard, willing the driver to hurry along. During the long route back to the boat harbor, I considered Tuna Lady's ramblings.

Adam and the Mojo-Jumbies

Tuna Lady's manic ramblings were part of a Vodou belief system. Voodoo or Vodou were more widely referred to as the modern practice of Obeah, practiced throughout the Caribbean.

Obeah is a term referred to as the use of sorcery and folk magic, associated with both benign and malignant magic, charms, luck and mysticism. The practice was introduced by African slaves and directed against the European slave masters. After the abolishment of slavery, Obeah was considered taboo, but still practiced.

One aspect of Obeah that is familiar to Caribbean adventurists are the Moko-Jumbies or the stilts walkers. During the St Thomas Carnival in the US Virgin Islands, the Moko-Jumbie characters donned colorful garb and masks to dance in street parades. We watched wide-eyed as they deftly waltzed by as we huddled beneath porticos on the main street of St Thomas. Jumbie means ghost, so I couldn't help but feel a wisp of chilly air as they strutted by.

In the traditional sense, the Moko was considered a god who watched over his village. Due to his towering height, he was able to foresee danger and evil. Moko literally means the 'diviner'.

He was able to perform unexplainable acts to the human eye.

The Moko arrived in the Caribbean by 'walking' all the way across the Atlantic Ocean from the West coast of Africa, laden with centuries of experience. Despite inhuman attacks, the Moko stilt walker was very tall. He survived by living in the hearts of African descendants during slavery.

Today, Moko characters walk the streets of Caribbean nations during Carnival in a celebration of freedom. He walks the streets to protect the city and revelers from evil. Onlookers in upper floors of buildings tossed down coins to donate to the Moko-Jumbie's cause, expecting good luck or a blessing.

10
TURTLE JUMP-UP

Turtle Hatchlings

Life is too beautiful to live it in your head.

—*Rainey*

It was time for my daily swim. Gazing into turquoise waters as clear as cellophane, I peered into depths for any hidden predators, surprised to see a 3" long, green turtle hatchling finning off the beam of *Scud*. Its tiny flippers paddled with grace, little ripples of water spinning off the tail.

A threatening screech came from overhead and I gazed up in horror to see a seagull bee-lining for the little fella. My heart pounded in my throat. Shaking my fist at the feathery beast, I shouted, "No!"

Suddenly, I was soaring mid-air, racing against the gull and time itself.

To do what exactly? Interfere with nature? Who really ponders scientific questions at a time like this? Gulls aren't endangered; sea turtles are!

As luck would have it, both gull and turtle vanished by the time I surfaced. I'll never know what happened to my little reptilian friend.

———•◦•———

We were anchored off Oranjestad in Aruba, the Netherland Antilles, roughly 475 nautical miles due west of Grenada or a mere 15 nautical miles due north of the Paraguaná Peninsula of Venezuela.

On the beach, Peter and I stood amongst a gaggle of onlookers, gazing at a clutch of 85 turtle hatchlings. The tiny turtles fought their way out of a hole in the sand, writhing and tumbling, a bubbly mass of flippers and heads. Scarlet ribbons placed by onlookers cut a swath of sand, marking a runway to the water's edge as if a Hollywood starlet's début. I half imagined Julia Roberts to come striding along.

Nearby, two erudite volunteer naturalists stood by with watchful eyes. They strolled along the beaches daily, alert for any sign of recent turtle hatchling activity.

In a furious flailing of tiny flippers, the hatchlings raced for the ocean, using an inborn compass to find their way. Some say the hatchling is crawling away from the land's higher horizon that directs them; others say it's because the water is brighter than the shore. If a turtle straggler wandered past the scarlet ribbons beneath the feet of the tourists, one of the naturalists gently prodded it back on course.

At the water's edge, the same hungry gull swooped down for supper, but the crowd succeeding in frightening it away with a resounding clap of hands or an impassioned yell.

Finally, all the turtles became waterborne, each successive wave having pulled them into the ocean. After this trek to the ocean, the hatchlings will ride ocean currents up the Atlantic coast, spending from three to five years in the deep waters.

The hatchlings are rarely seen in these early stages of life. As carnivores, they subsist on pelagic crustaceans like squid, jellyfish, and algae. Later, when returning to the shallow lagoons as immature juveniles, they settle into a more herbivorous, shallow-water lifestyle, feeding on sea-grasses and seaweed.

So the little fella beside my boat that auspicious day was cruising by, en route towards the US East Coast to begin a circumnavigation of the Atlantic basin, following ocean currents.

To breed, my reptilian friend may journey roughly 2,600 kilometers between her feeding grounds and Aruba, the original nesting site. Individual green turtles have been seen as far north as Canada and as far south as the southern tip of Africa and Argentina, even Ascension Island in the mid-Atlantic Ocean (you can only get there by fin or boat).

Female turtles return to the same nesting beach to lay their eggs, laying not more than 100 to a clutch, returning every two to four years after breeding. In Aruba or other Caribbean waters, nesting season is from June until September when the weather is hot and moist for incubation.

To prepare her nest, a female turtle drags herself up a wide beach above the high-tide line (to avoid flooding), to dig a hole with hind flippers and deposit her clutch. Hind flippers cover them with sand and she returns to the sea.

After 45 - 75 days, the eggs hatch, usually under the darkness of the night to avoid predators. It was unusual to see these hatchlings during daylight hours. The naturalist on site told us it was probably due to being an extremely cloudy day, during the low light of a late afternoon sun: it was 6:00PM.

The only known predators of the adult green turtle are humans and sharks. Many sea turtles die in fishing nets without TEDs (turtle exclusion devices) and others are killed when they eat ocean garbage, all too easily dropped over the side of boats.

The pretty black and-yellow plates on the back of hawksbill sea turtles were long sought for tortoiseshell jewelry and combs, now illegal. Other sea turtles are also killed to make leather products.

In Southeast Asia and China, turtles are both eaten and used in traditional medicine. A greatly increased Asian turtle trade in recent years has brought many formerly common species to the brink of extinction in this region.

The good news is: in the Caribbean, private resorts are making concerted efforts at conserving their beaches for returning female turtles. Tourists want to see them.

Eco-tourism saved the nesting beach of Tortuguero in Costa Rica. During the 1950s, thousands of eggs were harvested, either sold for money or eaten as food by poor villagers.

When the Tortuguero National Park was formed an entire village rose from the once deserted beach. Meaningful jobs had replaced the lucrative sale of turtle eggs, once a major source of income for the villagers.

Eyeing the last hard-shell hatchling enter the ocean waters, I wished my little friend good luck and happy endings.

—————••••————

Now, whenever a turtle surfaces and flashes me those liquid brown eyes, my heart swells. I feel blessed. I know one more adult turtle has made it back. Looking at such beauty in the water, I vow to do my best at conservation by educating others, boycotting shops that sell tortoiseshell items as well as restaurants that sell turtle meat.

11
THE SAN BLAS ISLANDS

Kuna Women Selling Molas

We travel not to escape life, but for life not to escape us.
Anonymous

I was walking my dog along a beach in Prickly Bay in Grenada when a cruiser chatted me up one morning a while back. My husband, Peter of 35 years, and I sailed aboard "Scud", a St. Francis 42' catamaran.

After an initial introductory conversation, she learned we had reared our two sons aboard, cruising the Caribbean waters between Venezuela and the Bahamas for several summers. As a last hurrah, we sailed with them around the world, ending up back in the Caribbean.

"So what's your favorite island in the Caribbean after having seen the world?"

"The San Blas," I said right away.

"Why?"

"It's magical, lost in distant time, unspoiled by modern society," I say. I couldn't believe we were having this conversation. Pandemonium ensued. How did she not see it? "Say, you mind calling off your dogs?"

"Oh, right. Sorry. They're just puppies; only six months old."

Puppies are useless when it comes to discipline. Kinda' like us when rearing our kids aboard a boat. Chaos, most of the time.

In time, Betsy distracted her dogs by throwing a tennis ball. They darted down the beach for their next hapless victim while we continued to chat. Soon, I found myself waxing on about the San Blas Islands, happy to be rid of the devils. I put Bella down, straightened my attire, and began to describe my idea of paradise.

"So what's the San Blas like?" she said.

"It's like no other place on earth. It's otherworldly, in a way. When we were there, it was as if we were on another planet," I said.

The San Blas islands were home to the native Guna Yala tribe, more widely known as the Kuna Indians. The women wear hand-stitched molas and colorful scarves. Beaded bands in hues of green, yellow, and orange encapsulate arms and legs. It's an impressive style to behold, more like a native American Indian than Madonna.

We first arrived at Cayos Diablo in the San Blas in 1979 aboard the "Antilles", a 47-foot Sparkman Stevens wooden ketch. It was a beat from Port Antonio, Jamaica to the archipelago. At that time, tourists were not permitted ashore without the permission of the caicique–the village chief.

No other boat arrived during the duration of our two-month stay. When back in Jamaica before our departure, word on the coconut run offered sage advice. "Don't even think about disobeying the caicique," a raconteur at the bar said in hushed tones. "My buddy swam ashore to one of the islands for a little socializing with the sheilas. Minutes later, he beat back waters in Olympian strokes as a fleet of arrows chased his tail. I kid you not."

Course that was back in the late 70's. And little wonder the Kunas threatened him. They are fiercely protective of their pubescent girls.

We were hesitant to explore ashore, respecting their privacy. Instead, we remained anchored off uninhabited islands, snorkeling the reef where scarlet lionfish–looking like flamenco dancers– pink goatfish, and schools of striped grunts darted about the coral. Waters were as clear as gin and lunching in the cockpit beneath clear blue skies, sea breezes wafted. On them rode the sweet scent of frangipani, date palms, and seaweed. The picturesque scenes were worthy of Van Gogh's touch.

At twilight, the sunset cast shadows that were deep and long. Colors blazed with pinks and reds in invisible love darts as the orange orb sank into the sea. We were newlyweds, oblivious to time and space.

When darkness fell, the moon was so bright, it cast beams of light upon starfish the size of basketballs on the sea floor alongside the boat. Ashore, moonlight washed waters in shimmering silver, illuminating a small reef near shore. Beneath palm fronds, moon shadows danced lacy patterns across sands.

One day while napping on deck beneath a canvas awning, a pod of bottle-nosed dolphins gamboled around the bow, squeaking in low-pitched tones. Around us, we watched transfixed as pelicans dive-bombed for juvenile blue runners. In the distance, the traditional wooden craft of the Kuna's sailed in on a sea breeze, their tiny white sails resembling flickers of candles.

We heard them one morning before we saw them. Fits of giggles rode the morning breeze as sunlight streaked through hatches, drawing me awake. We leaned on elbows to peer out the aft cabin port hole. A *cayucos* or dugout was gliding across still waters, low on the waterline with a gaggle of women.

Clambering on deck, we sat atop the coach roof to spy their approach. Tiny brown fingers trolled the waters, dangling alongside the dugout. In the binoculars, I smiled when a naked toddler with curly brown hair came into view. He peeked above the laps between two women who were donned in traditional garb. Giggling ensued even louder as the party advanced. The combination of their natural beauty against turquoise waters drove me to near tears.

"Buenos dias," I said when they reached up to grab our rub rail.

The women continued to smile, nod, and giggle. It became apparent they did not speak Spanish. Instead, they spoke Dulegaya, I later learned.

In sign language, they mimed their intention: the sale of molas. They held up ten fingers, signaling that each mola cost $10. At such a bargain, I bought several. They adorn my boat today.

The mola is a colorful panel of hand-stitched art, crafted in reverse applique. This panel is sewn into a blouse as front and back panels. A wrapped skirt or *saburet* and a headscarf called a *musue* completes the outfit. A gold nose ring or *olaus* and earrings called *dulemor* accessorize the look.

Initially, the Kuna women painted their bodies in geometric designs with plant dies until the European settlers arrived from Panama bearing gifts of cotton broadcloth. Today, the same designs were used in creating the panels.

To understand the Kunas, you need to know where and how they gained autonomy. First of all, the San Blas archipelago encompasses 100 square miles and consist of 378 islands. It is a semi-autonomous region of Panama. The indigenous people, the Kuna Yala, have had contact with Europeans since the 1600s. As a consequence, they are fiercely independent.

In 1924, they violently rose up against the Panamanian government in response to adverse policies affecting them. As shrewd diplomats, the Kuna Yala struck a deal with the American military, nearby in the Canal Zone.

When Panamanian military elements moved to respond to the uprising, a Yankee gunboat waited for them. Backed by the Americans and powered with a deep sense of sovereignty, the Kuna Yala negotiated a constitution with the Panamanians. Subsequent constitutions have ceded more autonomy to the Kuna Yala. Today, the Kuna have their own governance and police force. Little wonder that they were able to hold onto their passionate lifestyle. It resonated with me.

After the women in the dugout departed, the fleet of small tradi-tional craft that I had seen the day before, sailed into view. Eventually, they landed on the beach in front of us. Short brown men spilled out of gunnels and sprinted up palm trees to gather coconuts. When their wooden boats were filled at sunset, they departed in their wooden craft, rub rails low on the water. Coconuts are the sole cash crop for the Kunas. It is forbidden for sailors to collect coconuts. Still, I was dying to prepare ceviche with coconut milk.

The last night of our stay, a conch horn blew, signaling a feast. It was soon accompanied by Andean pipes and beating drums. I fingered the *chakira* or beaded anklet, thick with beads, that I had purchased from the Kuna women. I considered the music a parting gift, an augury of great things to come. Tomorrow we were en route to the Panama Canal and needed all the good vibes we could muster.

Today, the San Blas are thriving with tourism as backpackers arrive on fast boats to fill makeshift hostels. It's still a magical paradise but I was pleased we had visited decades earlier, before their slow segue into modern times with Honda generators and cell phones.

12
SUNSET BLISS

An Uninhabited Island

You must love in such a way that the person you love feels free.

Thich Nhat Hanh

The wooden dinghy drifted to shore as Peter stroked the waters with oars. His muscles glistened in the sunlight, and I smiled, taking my sweetheart in. A liquid rush soared up my veins, and I held onto it with genuine pleasure.

My heart alighted when we rounded a rocky bend to find pink sand carpeting a remote beach. Against the backdrop of a distant horizon, the beach lay fringed in swaying palms. A whisper rode the summer breeze as fronds swished in rhythmic tones. As we approached the beach, the bow of the little boat parted waters, sending a ripple of tiny rainbows skittering across the harbor. All around us floated a carpet of sparkling diamonds that winked at us in brilliant sunlight.

We were anchored in the San Blas Islands where its intended promise of beauty held true.

We alighted from the dinghy, pulling it up to the high water mark to ensure we still had a dinghy when we returned. More than once I've jumped into the sea to retrieve a drifting dinghy. Swimming in these waters at dusk into an open roadstead didn't feel particularly appealing.

As we headed towards the sun to explore the island, sugary sand felt soft beneath my feet. An occasional piece of driftwood littered the pristine beach. Overhead, sea birds circled the tops of palms, preparing to roost for the night. A cacophony of nesting birds reverberated from the thick canopy. Now and then, a bird swooped upon the waters in search of prey.

When we came upon the dark outline of a reef, we donned our mask and snorkel to quietly ease into the waters. Best not to announce yourself right away with a loud splash, lest beastly bulls come calling—the bull sharks. Bulls like to sneak up on you when you least expect it. I had to fend off a couple of bulls once before, and the memory will be forever etched in my mind.

As we entered the reef, waters were warm and clear as mountain air down to the seafloor. We finned to the outer reef and found golden brain coral standing sentinel next to stately stalks of elkhorn coral, reaching towards the sky like witches' claws. A little damselfish in hues of blue with electric lights darted about a coral cave, warning off intruders. I finned down to take a closer look. The tiny fish grew annoyed with my presence and charged my face mask, flexing muscle. I smiled at its bravery.

Soft corals lay scattered around the hard corals. I finned down to engage with a lavender sea anemone. I fanned my hand above tubes of silk and giggled as they jetted back into its coral base. Atop the waters, I watched as the pretty tubes slowly emerged to writhe in the current.

Other tropical fish flitted about in the light current. Brilliant butterfly fish in vibrant yellows, the black-and-white striped jackknife, and assorted squirrel fish in scarlet hues. The magic of the reef soothed my soul. My heart swelled in appreciation of the beauty.

I heard a whistle and looked to see Peter pointing below. I followed him down to a coral patch where he pointed out the tell-tale signs of a lobster: long swaying antennas resembling twigs. Peter cocked a Hawaiian sling, took a deep breath, and finned down. Pulling back, he released the cup to send the spear on a direct target for the crayfish. Bam! Right between the eyes. The lobster was large enough to feed two people.

"Way to go, babe!" I shouted when he surfaced.

Satiated and ready for dinner, we finned towards shore. There, Peter released a clasp from his ankle to free a large knife. He cleaned the lobster by removing the carapace and saving the tail. In the meantime, I collected kindling and dried fronds to start a small fire.

As the smoke swirled above the fire, Peter placed the lobster tail on the embers, and we sat down to wait. The sun began to edge toward the sea, and Peter reached over to slowly untie my bikini strings. "Let's take one last dip before the tail is ready," he said.

Peter stripped as well, and we lowered our bare bodies into the lagoon. Waters cast colorful shadows as the sky turned into a myriad shade of pinks, blues, and reds. Peter stretched his arms out over the water and coaxed me into them. He floated me around across the shallows as if I were a raft. Magic spilled all around us. I felt love fill my veins like liquid gold and I reveled in it. I smiled towards the heavens, thanking God and Earth for my blessings.

In time, we eased out of dark waters and sat next to the fire pit. We eased supine upon the sands. Peter took me in his arms and time drifted away as darkness fell.

Just before the water and sky met as one, Peter reached for the hot lobster tail, now blackened nicely, and ripped it open with his trusty knife. Feeding steaming bites into my mouth, I tasted salty flesh and smiled.

I am still smiling.

13
Become A Minimalist

The Dreffin Family

Minimalism is living with what you need and what you love. No more. No less.

—Tina Dreffin

That'll be $40," the pretty barmaid said to my new cruising girl buddy, Lyla, who rumbled around in her knapsack for the required funds. I handed over my share of the $2.00 for my Diet Coke. Inside the "Happy People" café, we'd been sharing our cruising yarns of having crossed the Anegada Passage with our husbands for the first time, watching the colorful crowd come and go. New to cruising, their crossing had been a particularly bumpy one, but with her spirit being like that of an eagle, I knew she'd adapt well, although her cruising adventures looked as if they may be a short one. So far, her consumer habits seemed more conducive to a working woman, than that of a cruiser.

"How long do you think you'll be out cruising?" I asked Lyla.

"About year, when the cruising kitty goes," she replied.

As a bluewater cruiser for nearly thirty years, I've seen the same tale over and over again. New cruisers embrace the new cruising life as high rollers their first year or two. They eat out in expensive restaurants, buy things they don't need, and generally throw money around like it grows on trees. After a year or two, they are forced to return to the workforce, and end up selling their boat. Such a short time for a dream that took years to arrange. My husband and I relish our new cruising friendships. We'd like to see them stay out longer.

Here are a few tips to first-timers. My husband calls it, "Becoming a minimalist". It may require adopting a Buddha nature to learn to become unattached to STUFF, but with diligence and self-discipline, you'll find the end is worth it.

1. Eat on the boat at home, instead of in restaurants. Use new spices and produce grown on the island to create zest in your food preparation.

2. Invite friends over for a potluck. In every new port, we try to arrange either potluck sundowners or dinners, where everyone brings their own favorite dish and beverage. Being the host and doing clean-up duty afterwards, is my part in bringing new friends together, which they greatly appreciate.

3. Another option instead of dining in restaurants is to arrange a picnic on a sheet next to a brook in the rain forest or on the beach. It's fun, and rarely practiced anymore. Friends say, "That was a great idea!"

4. Shop in farmers' markets, instead of supermarkets. It's far more fun to chat up a produce merchant in the market stalls. Often it's a grandmother or mother, who relishes passing down family recipes to prepare the new foodstuff you've just bargained over.

5. Cut down on alcohol, an expensive item, or at least moderate your intake. If you add up your weekly booze bill, you'll find it may have become higher than the food bill, simply because partying is such a part of the cruising culture. It doesn't have to be. Adopt measures and stick by them. You'll be far healthier in the end.

6. Never grocery shop on an empty stomach. I've seen myself buy out the whole store, when half starving to death. Eat before you go. You'd be shocked how low your bill can get.

7. Always take a list to the marine stores. Ask yourself, "Do I need this or do I just want it?" Put back the 'want' on the shelf and forget about it. The but, but, buts can go on forever.

8. Take a bag sandwich on island tours, along with a liter of water; otherwise, you'll find yourself picking your pockets for another unanticipated meal. This works especially well with children. You can better control their diet; they're always hungry. A granola bar and sandwich is much healthier than fried chicken from a road stall.

9. For repairs, try to have them done in ports where you know the tradesmen are well-trained. Ask around. Often, you can be stuck hauled out, waiting for marina repairs that don't seem to ever come. We've known of friends hauled out on the hard for two months, while waiting for repairs to START. Talk to a cruiser who has hauled before at the same marina, who can attest to their integrity. Confirm the time and date that work will commence. It if hasn't within a sensible frame of time, don't hang around.

10. Invite family and close friends from home to visit you, instead of you flying out to visit them. Your boat has to be safe and cared for at a marina or on a mooring, further reaching into your pocket, when you depart. When your loved ones visit, take them grocery shopping on the first day and split the bill. Putting them up during their say is an act of grace, but assuming all expenses is not expected or necessary. All our old-time cruising friends have adopted this practice after their first years of agonizing monetary pain, seeing their cruising budget diminish in a very short time by hosting loved ones. Once your family understands the practice of visiting on your boat, they'll visit more often, freeing you up to not only enjoy their stay more, but allowing you to remain cruising just a little bit longer.

ABOUT TINA DREFFIN

Croc Viewing on the Great Barrier Reef, Australia

Tina Dreffin is an accomplished travel writer, world sailor and circumnavigator, and an advocate for women's issues. She moved aboard her first boat in 1979, and raised two sons, now grown, aboard various sailing vessels.

Tina Dreffin is author of *Bluewater Walkabout: Into Africa,* available as an eBook, in paperback, and in audio format. Simply download the Kindle app to read on any device. Her photography and articles appear in several magazines, including *Cruising World, SAIL, International Living, Multihulls Magazine, Multihull Sailor,* and the *Caribbean Compass.* She has also had work included in the anthology *The Best of the Caribbean Compass.*

You may view the route of her world circumnavigation: http://bahamascatcharters.com/family_circumnavigation.htm.

Tina currently lives aboard a catamaran in the Bahamas with her husband, and a Belgium barge dog named Bella–a Schipperke. Bella is known for her wild antics of swimming with Nikki, the wild dolphin. You can view the YouTube video of the *Dog and Dolphin Wrestle* here: https://youtu.be/k3Ixow3NfyE.

Wild Dolphin Nikki Teasing Bella

Tina's sons now own their own sailing catamarans. Together they operate a licensed family yacht charter business in the Exumas, Bahamas where the famous swimming pigs reside on White Cay Bay nearby.

Book your next vacation with world renown chef, Tina Dreffin here: http://www.bahamascatcharters.com.

Family Fleet

Tina's travels aren't limited to the sea. She and her family have traveled the world by train, donkey, horseback, bicycle, and plane. She hosts presentations of her photography and works as a motivational speaker, encouraging families to travel with their children, put down their devices, and get out and explore.

To learn of Tina Dreffin's forthcoming books in the series of Bluewater Walkabout, drop your email address here for personal updates: http://www.bluewaterwalkabout.com.

Email: tinadreffin@bluewaterwalkabout.com
Websites:
www.tinacarlsondreffin.com
www.bluewaterwalkabout.com
www.bahamascatcharters.com
Tina Dreffin's Social Networks

Phone: WhatsApp: 1-242-524-0156
Tina Dreffin
6501 Redhook Plaza, Ste. #201
St Thomas, US Virgin Islands 00802-1306

Made in the USA
Columbia, SC
17 December 2020